SHIRE  ALBUM

Vintage Tractors

CHARLES L. CAWOOD

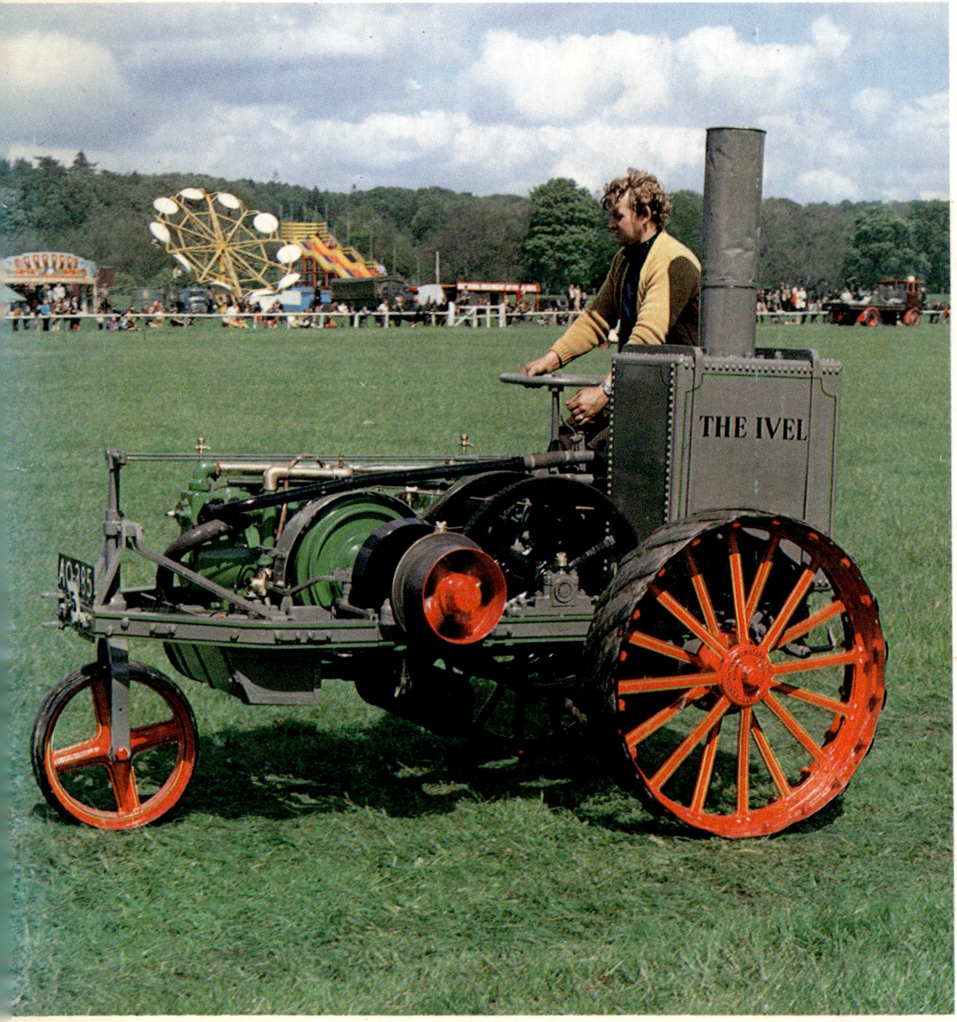

David Brown Cropmaster diesel, the first David Brown diesel tractor model (1949). The advanced design of the four-cylinder direct injection engine with its instant starting and good fuel economy quickly won the enthusiastic approval of farmers — and began the decline in popularity of the kerosene engine.

INTRODUCTION

Tractors are an essential part of farming today; if they disappeared, the world would soon starve. But the replacement of horses by tractors took engineers and farsighted farmers many years of endeavour and frustration.

The first tractor was made in the United States in 1889 and the Americans pioneered the commercial use of tractors. By 1910 at least ten thousand tractors were working in the USA and Canada, whereas in Britain, where, because labour was cheap and plentiful, there was no incentive to change, the number was probably under fifty. But the First World War provided the incentive and by 1916 tractors were appearing on farms in small numbers. By 1921 twenty thousand were working in Britain. The disastrous agricultural slump of 1921-2 and the Depression of 1929-34 rendered progress slow, but gradually tractors increased their influence until by the outbreak of war in 1939 there were around fifty-five thousand tractors in Britain. The requirement for home-grown food during the Second World War stimulated demand to such an extent that the number of tractors quadrupled and it has gone on growing ever since. The working farm horse has become a curiosity.

After a short look at the early history of the tractor, this book traces its growth and development from the British point of view from the First World War to the end of the 'vintage period' in the mid 1950s.

The term 'tractor' is used to mean a self-propelled machine, primarily intended to pull, carry or drive other implements, machines and vehicles used in agriculture, and powered by an internal combustion engine. A 'vintage tractor' is one that was on the market before 1952. This is an arbitrary date but is chosen mainly because it marks the beginning of the diesel age on the farm.

ABOVE: *The Charter (1889) was the first petrol-engined tractor ever to be built. It was made by John Charter, a pioneer of the gasoline engine industry in the USA, and consisted basically of a large 20 hp (15 kW) single-cylinder open crank petrol engine crudely assembled on parts of a Rumely steam traction engine. Apparently it was quite successful and about six were made and placed on farms in North Dakota.*
BELOW: *Very little information on Petters tractors has come to light, but this one, named Intrepid, was their first and most probably one of the first half dozen tractors to be made in Europe. Built in 1896-7, it was powered by a large single-cylinder oil engine and was followed, up to 1915, by a succession of various models, all oil-engined and all commercial failures, surprising for such a forward looking and otherwise successful company.*

The Huber was the world's first 'production' tractor, thirty being built in 1898. It was virtually a replica of the 1894 Van Duzen, whose patents the Huber Company bought. The single-cylinder vertical engine with hot tube ignition developed about 25 hp (19 kW) at the very slow rate of about 325 rpm. The transmission and running gear were an adaptation of the standard American practice with steam traction engines, Huber being large-scale makers of these and threshers.

THE EARLIEST TRACTORS

The first tractor on record was built in Chicago in 1889 and was called the Charter. Others followed in the 1890s, including British models by Petters of Yeovil and Hornsby of Grantham, both in 1896, but most of the very small production of this era was American. In 1898 the Huber Company of Marion, Ohio, produced thirty machines (the first production run) and in 1899 the Kinnard-Haines Company of Minneapolis made twenty-seven.

In 1902-3 an Englishman, Dan Albone of Biggleswade, produced a revolutionary design of lightweight tractor, the Ivel, specifically designed for general farm work, which was to influence many other designers, and another Englishman, H. P. Saunderson, was also making tractors of novel design. Few very early tractors have survived but there are two 1904 Ivels in England and a Hornsby of 1897 has been found in Australia.

By 1906-7 several firms, among them Ivel and Saunderson, were establishing a foothold in the market; perhaps the largest were the International Harvester Company of Chicago, still a major manufacturer today, and the Hart-Parr Company of Charles City, Iowa, where tractors are still made in the same factory by the White Company. These pioneers were followed in the years up to 1914 by many others, both producers and experimenters, including Henry Ford, who made some 'bodge ups' in 1907, and J. M. Eason of Topeka, Kansas. Both, like Dan Albone, worked against the general trend

The prototype model of the famous Ivel, made in 1902 and shown with its designer, Dan Albone, driving. Its compact lightweight design and obvious handiness provide an interesting contrast with the lumbering contemporary American tractors. This model differs from the production model shown on the cover mainly in its transmission, which is friction drive in reverse and chain drive in the forward gear, whereas the later types were chain drive forward and gear drive reverse. It also lacks provision for a belt pulley, which was provided on the later version.

of heavyweight design, more akin to steam traction engine size and weight, to make smaller, nimbler and more generally useful tractors. In 1907 a Frenchman, M. Gougis, made and successfully demonstrated a tractor *driving* a towed implement by direct engine power through a universally jointed shaft; this was the birth of the power take-off (PTO), which eventually became essential equipment on tractors.

By 1914 the trend in tractors was away from the massive, slow and clumsy machines of former years. Although they survived for many years longer, the mass market was swinging to lighter, smaller and handier machines, as advocated by Albone ten years before. In 1913 the Bull tractor appeared in the USA. Of extraordinary design but light weight, it immediately set sales records, and the International Harvester Company produced two crude but simple and reliable low-powered tractors that were to serve farmers well for many years: the Mogul 8-16 and the even more famous and popular Titan 10-20. Many Titans were imported to Britain near the end of the First World War and after, and some were still working as late as the Second World War.

The American-built Wallis Cub was the most important new design of the period before 1914. Designed, in part, by J. M.

ABOVE: *The production Ivel ploughing. Its steam pipe and exhaust pipe are to the driver's left. The thicker steam pipe is to take water vapour away from the cooling tank and also to prevent water splashing on to the driver. The bonnet (hood) is in position, but these were seldom used in practice, being awkward and heavy to handle when servicing, until a modified sliding bonnet appeared around 1910.*
BELOW: *The Gougis tractor of 1906-7 was the first in the world to use a universally jointed power take-off shaft to drive trailed machines directly by engine power, in this case a McCormick binder. The tractor is very like the Ivel but has a four-cylinder in-line petrol engine. A highly successful prototype, it was before its time and was eventually developed by International Harvester in America in the early 1920s. The French firm (now Nodet-Gougis) still survives and makes precision seed drills.*

ABOVE: *This is the first production model of International Harvester Company tractor, the 10-20 of 1906. Only the engine, a large horizontal single-cylinder, was of IHC manufacture, the chassis and friction drive transmission being purchased from the Ohio Manufacturing Company, which took over the Morton patents of 1899 and also supplied several other engine makers, such as Stover and Alamo, with chassis. Two hundred Internationals of this model were built before the transmission was altered to gear drive.*

TOP LEFT: *This is one of the six or so 'bodge ups' made by Henry Ford, seen driving, and Joe Galamb in 1907 to test the practicality of Ford's ideas for a lightweight tractor and which led, indirectly, to the famous Fordson of 1917, with the design of which Galamb assisted.*

BOTTOM LEFT: *Manufactured from 1910 to 1922, the Aultman and Taylor 30-60 is an example of a typical American high-powered prairie tractor, more resembling a traction engine in construction, size and weight than a normal tractor. The Aultman and Taylor Company, of Canton, Ohio, was a long-time maker of high-class steam traction engines and threshing machines, and its tractors, which first came on the market in 1910, were regarded as the Rolls-Royces of heavy tractors. Powered by a horizontal four-cylinder overhead valve petrol paraffin engine capable of developing 90 hp (67 kW), the 30-60 lasted until the firm was taken over by the Advance-Rumely Company in 1924.*

Eason, it established the principles of total enclosure and frameless construction. All previous tractors had chassis frames built up from steel sections and the engine, gearbox and final drive units were bolted to it, allowing opportunity for distortion and misalignment and for dust to enter the vitals of the 'openwork' engines, gearboxes and back axles. The Wallis Cub prevented that by making the engine, gearbox and rear axle fit into a half-round 'trough' of heavy steel plate, which, when fitted, was sealed against dust and partly filled with oil; thus the chassis was eliminated, the trough having taken its place, and the working parts were totally enclosed. So the basic design of tractors of the future was born; the principle survives on most tractors today.

This photograph illustrates the generally used method of construction of tractors before the totally enclosed frameless machines like the Wallis, Fordson and Fiat became widely used. It illustrates a tractor chasis of 1914 without engine and wheels, showing how crude methods were in this period and in some cases for many years after.

This advertisement of 1917 shows the popular IHC Mogul 8-16 and Titan 10-20 tractors which were used in quantity in Britain during and after the First World War. 3500 Titans and over 1300 small Moguls came over and proved to be good and reliable tractors. The Titan especially became a byword for excellence, many working right up to the 1940s. Both models were introduced in 1913-14, the Mogul being superseded in 1918 by the IHC Junior and the Titan giving place to the McCormick-Deering 10-20 in 1923.

We Guarantee Mogul and Titan Tractors To Operate On Kerosene

In spite of the fact that for some years past Mogul and Titan tractors have operated successfully on kerosene in the hands of average farmers, we still find a vague doubt in the minds of many possible tractor dealers and buyers that any internal combustion tractor will operate successfully and continuously on kerosene.

It is not difficult to find the source of this doubt. The issue is one upon which few people except trained engineers have any definite data. The average farmer, untrained in technical engineering theory or practice, might easily be swayed from one side to another by the plausible talk of clever salesmen.

We found it necessary to devise a simple, not to be misunderstood method of proving that Mogul and Titan tractors would operate successfully on kerosene in all ordinary circumstances. In order to remove the last shadow of doubt from the mind of any man who was wavering between buying a Mogul or Titan or a gasoline tractor, because he was not sure that our tractors would live up to the promises made for them, we incorporated in the warranty which goes to every purchaser of one of our tractors a definite guarantee that Mogul and Titan tractors would operate successfully on kerosene.

We wish to emphasize the statement that the above guarantee applies to all of the Mogul and Titan tractors described on pages 51 to 53.

International Harvester Company of America
(Incorporated)

Chicago   U. S. A.

This Wallis OK model clearly shows the Wallis frameless arrangement, using a rolled steel 'trough' on which the front axle, engine, gearbox and final drive were mounted, to give a total dustproof enclosure. This system was originated in cruder form on the Wallis Cub of 1913 and was used only by Wallis, their licensees, Ruston and Hornsby, and their successors, the Massey Harris Company up to 1939. It was the pioneer of all unit-construction frameless tractors.

THE FIRST WORLD WAR

On the outbreak of war in 1914 the American tractor industry was quietly flourishing and the British industry consisted of three main firms, Ivel, Saunderson and Marshall, which exported nearly all their production to the colonies; the European industry barely existed. But by 1917 the war had destroyed the British industry, with the exception of Saunderson, and the Americans were producing tractors in immense numbers.

Britain was dependent on America for its food supplies and German U boats had brought the country to the verge of starvation. The only hope was to increase food production at home, which up to then had been neglected, the land having been deprived of both men and horses for service on the Western Front. The only solution was to mechanise agriculture and this meant importing tractors; because of the shortage of shipping a cargo of tractors had more potential value than one of wheat or beef. But, although the established American manufacturers had hitherto met the increased demand from both their own and overseas markets, the type of tractor in current general production and the style of factories making them rendered a rapid increase in production virtually impossible, because the tractors of the period were not designed for mass production; they were built one at a time, with hand fitting of parts. An increase in production required a much larger and highly skilled labour force, which was not readily available, and a massive expansion of factory space, which could not be quickly achieved. The time was ripe for a new approach to tractors — for a rationalised and simplified design, made to conform to the

ABOVE: *Marshall of Gainsborough, well known for steam traction engines and threshing machines, entered the tractor field with this two-cylinder petrol paraffin model in 1907. Designed by H. W. Bamber of London, it soon gave way to larger versions, most of which were exported to Canada, Australia and southern Africa. One still exists in a museum in Saskatchewan. Very heavy, crude and clumsy, they were fairly typical of prairie tractors of the period. Production ceased sometime during the First World War and was not resumed until the Marshall 15-30 single-cylinder two-stroke diesel appeared in 1930. The firm now makes only crawler tractors.*

BELOW: *The Bull, called the Whiting Bull in Britain, was the first big-selling tractor in 1913. Of unusual design, with one large wheel running in the furrow when ploughing, one wheel steering and one wheel to stop it falling over, the original Little Bull became the Big Bull shown because it lacked power. The later model had auxiliary drive to the small balancing rear wheel and a two-cylinder horizontally opposed 20 hp (15 kW) engine.*

ABOVE: *An Overtime, or Waterloo Boy, ploughing in the First World War. These crude two-cylinder American-built tractors were imported to Britain in considerable numbers between 1917 and 1920 and proved popular and reliable machines. Although even then their design was outdated, with their slow-revving paraffin engine, open gear final drive and fifth-wheel traction-engine type steering, their robust construction made then the productivity record holders of 1918. John Deere purchased the firm that same year and continued to make them with some modifications until 1923, when the first John Deere tractor was announced, the famous Model D.*
BELOW: *An Emerson Brantingham of 1917 shown at a demonstration. This clearly shows an early type of mechanically lifted mounted plough. It was probably this kind of machine which inspired Harry Ferguson. Emerson Brantingham persevered longer than any firm with mounted implements on these general lines but eventually were taken over by the Case Company in 1928, after which the idea lapsed until the advent of the Ferguson tractor in 1936.*

ABOVE: *This Avery tractor made in Peoria, Illinois, in 1917 illustrates the crude and obsolete design of the majority of tractors before the advent of the Fordson. Note the complete absence of any gear enclosure, leading to very rapid wear in the transmission, and the open clutch in the flywheel — this is a direct adaptation of American traction-engine design, as is the chain and barrel (fifth wheel) steering; like many after, this Avery is little more than a converted steam traction engine and as such could never be a really successful machine. The same remarks apply to its contemporaries, such as the Mogul, Overtime and Saunderson. All these designs were eventually swept away by the unit construction tractors of Ford, International, Fiat and others.*

BELOW: *One of the pre-production prototypes of the Fordson, clearly showing the cast iron unit construction and the extreme simplicity.*

In 1917 Herbert, later Lord, Austin, apart from running his own large and thriving car and truck factory at Longbridge, Birmingham, was the agent in Britain for several makes of American tractor, including the strange-looking Bates Steel Mule half-track and the Killen-Strait, which in 1915 formed the basis for the very first tracked armoured fighting vehicle, later to become the tank. In 1918 he disposed of these interests and started to design his own tractor, which was essentially a copy of the Fordson but incorporated a transverse two-speed gearbox instead of Ford's in-line three-speed unit. It used a modified Austin 'Heavy 20' car engine, running on paraffin, and was considerably more refined and somewhat more powerful than the Fordson; it did not share the Fordson reliability however, being given to breaking crankshafts and other troubles, nor could it compete with Ford prices. After a brief success in 1919-24, when it proved to be the financial saviour of Austin's tottering post-war fortunes until the advent of the Austin 7 car, production was withdrawn to France, where production continued, in modified form and with only moderate success, until about 1932.

exigencies of conveyor-belt production and assembly by unskilled labour.

This approach to production had been mastered by Henry Ford with cars, and since early 1915 Ford's men had been working on tractor design to fulfil his ambition to dominate the tractor market as he dominated that for cars. When Britain needed tractors in 1917, Ford was the only man capable of supplying them in the necessary numbers at short notice. The desperate importunities of the British persuaded Ford to place his tractor in production, solely at first for the British government, in October 1917. The modern tractor had arrived; constructed as a unit like the Wallis, totally enclosed, light, handy and speedy, it was the most influential as well as the most commercially important design ever to come on the market. Eugene Farkas, the chief of design, had skilfully adapted the basic Wallis idea into a three-unit cast iron construction that still dominates conventional tractor design and has never been improved on. Three quarters of a million of these Fordsons were sold from 1917 to 1928, more than any other tractor before or since and at prices that seem ludicrous today, the lowest price in the USA being the equivalent of £75.

The Glasgow (1919-23) used Ford's cast iron unit construction, but there the resemblance ended. It had three-wheel drive and no differential, the front wheels having hub ratchets, so that in reverse it became a one-wheel drive. Quite highly thought of in its day, financial problems brought about its downfall and few were made.

The Fiat 702, their pioneer model of 1919, showing very clearly the three-piece cast iron chassisless construction, identical in principle to the 1917 Fordson, but in a 'Super de luxe' and very expensive form. The tractor shown has its mudguards and bonnet removed for clarity.

This photograph of an Irish-built Fordson Model F of 1919, taken at the SMMT Lincoln Tractor Trials in that year, shows the full production version of this famous tractor, with the early twelve-spoke rear wheels and 'ladder-side' radiator.

THE NINETEEN TWENTIES

When the war ended, Ford's prices put out of business the many manufacturers who had cashed in on the market between 1914 and 1920, and the fate of the old-fashioned slow-speed tractors like the Mogul, the Titan and the Overtime was sealed. Other makes had to conform just to remain in business. Herbert Austin in 1919 produced an indifferent copy of the Fordson, Fiat in Italy and Twin City in the USA superior ones. International Harvester, cautiously as always, by 1921 had started production of their 15-30, followed by the more famous 10-20, which were modifications of the basic Ford design, though much better made and much more expensive. It was on these tractors that the power take-off finally came into production, giving 'triple power', by traction, belt pulley and PTO.

In Britain after 1918 many tractor firms went into production, but few survived for long. One interesting design, the Glasgow, featured Ford's cast iron unit construction but was of three-wheeled layout with all wheels driven. Even Saunderson, once Britain's largest maker, went into liquidation; Austin withdrew to France, and Marshalls and many others ceased tractor manufacture. In the USA only those firms that were financially sound, well managed and possessed forward looking design staff survived for long the onslaught of the Fordson, and even they had to practise ruthless economy and price cutting to stay in business. But design steadily advanced and tractor use grew.

In Europe two designs appeared that were to have lasting influence. The German Lanz Bulldog came in 1921, with a single-cylinder two-stroke surface ignition engine, capable of burning many kinds of residual and waste oils, and in 1923 the Benz Company introduced the world's first diesel-engined tractor. The Bulldog, with its extreme simplicity, reliability and cheapness of running, immediately set a European standard for tractors that lasted until the mid 1950s. Firms in all continental countries either built Bulldogs under licence or made copies of it. Some, like Munktells of Sweden (now BM Volvo), made refined versions; but, in general, a booming exhaust note and a cloud of greasy smoke was the trademark of the European two-stroke oil-engined tractor. The Benz diesel, although a technical success, had to

ABOVE LEFT: *The Lanz Bulldog of 1921, which was basically a single-cylinder two-stroke blowlamp-start hopper-cooled stationary engine mounted on a chassis, came to be the prototype for many European tractors of the next thirty years. It had an immense capacity for hard work and great reliability, due to its massive construction, simplicity and good quality, and was not at all fussy about its fuel: it would digest, with equal facility, diesel oil, boiler fuel, paraffin, waste lubricating oil and almost any other hydrocarbon that could be poured into the tank. To the European farmer, the Bulldog was as important a milestone in tractor design as the Fordson was to the Americans and British. In modified and refined form the pattern of many makes, it survived into the mid 1950s, when it finally succumbed to the superior economy of the diesel proper.*

ABOVE RIGHT: *The famous and long-lived McCormick-Deering International 10-20 of 1923, with its semi-frameless construction and its two ball-bearing crankshafts, with its bigger brother, the 15-30 of 1921, set new standards of reliability and durability. By today's standards it was painfully slow and uncomfortable and liable to half-poison its driver by the fumes from its low-mounted exhaust, not to mention its cast iron steering wheel which stuck to one's fingers on cold mornings, but it was an extremely good tractor and well over 200,000 of them were produced between 1923 and 1940.*

wait many years before gaining wide acceptance, but it was a portent of the future.

In the USA design continued to advance. In 1924 International Harvester produced the Farmall, the first successful rowcrop tractor, designed to invade the last domain of the horse and mule, the cultivation of rowcrops (sugar beet, potatoes, cotton, maize and so on). Of tricycle layout, with a high clearance to pass over growing crops without damaging them, it could carry implements mounted underneath and to the rear. Easily manoeuvred, with its automatic steering brakes, it was ideally suited to its job. It could also perform more normal tractor tasks such as ploughing and cultivating and it proved a resounding sales success, being widely copied by other makers. Some had produced tractors that could work in rowcrops but none had the universal application of the Farmall. Its basic design, much refined survives still.

In Britain and the USA virtually all tractors used four or six cylinder high-speed (1200 rpm) engines burning refined paraffin and its variants and starting on petrol, in contrast to the European Bulldog type. Although costlier to run, they were more elegant than the crude, thumping Bulldogs. However, towards the end of the 1920s, the diesel became more popular, generally as a single-cylinder horizontal in both two and four stroke form. Mercedes Benz, Marshall, Deutz, Fendt and others started to use it in 1929-31 and the British Marshall two-stroke, though never made in large numbers, endured from 1930 to 1957 through various styles and models to become a much respected tractor and a favourite with collectors today. Garretts of Leiston in Suffolk also put a four-cylinder electric-start high-speed diesel-engined tractor on the market in 1930, but its price (£550) and the company's internal problems rendered it a commercial failure.

ABOVE: *Introduced in early 1916, the Saunderson Model G was by far the most successful of that firm's many types. Fairly crude, but simple and reliable, it became the most popular British-made tractor of its time, until Austin took over the premier position in 1920-1. By 1924 both Saunderson and Austin tractors were virtually unsalable, and Saunderson sold out to Crossley Brothers and Austin retired to France. A few more tractors were made to the same design under the Crossley name up to about 1931.*

BELOW: *This advertisement illustrates the original John Deere tricycle G-P (general-purpose) design of 1934, which was the first tractor to utilise hydraulic lift to its mid and rear mounted integral implements.*

TOP: *This was the world's first diesel-engined four-wheeled tractor, under its Benz Marienfelde name of 1923 onwards. It was preceded by a three-wheeled (single driver) model in 1922. It had a two-cylinder 850 rpm solid injection Benz diesel and although made in limited numbers it was without doubt the first production diesel. The example shown is a McLaren-Benz built under licence by J. and H. McLaren in Leeds in 1930. Probably less than three hundred were made, mostly for export.*
CENTRE: *The McCormick-Deering (IHC) Farmall was the culmination of many years of experimentation by IHC and other firms to design a tractor for all farmwork — not only primary cultivations, harvesting and so on, but to perform incrop cultivations as well, that is to work in the rows of growing crops, such as cotton, maize, sugar beet and potatoes. The Farmall, designed by Bert Benjamin, successfully and for the first time conbined into one tractor the ability to 'farm all' and its basic design has remained largely unchanged to this day.*
BOTTOM: *This was the revised and improved Fordson of 1929, produced in Cork, Irish Free State (now Eire), after production of the original Model F ceased in the USA in early 1928. The main differences were that this version had a slightly more powerful engine, high tension ignition, a water pump, mudguards as standard and heavier front wheels. About thirty-five thousand were made.*

The A-C Model U, originally produced as the United in 1928, became famous as the tractor chosen by Allis-Chalmers for publicising the then new air tyres in 1932-3. It was later imported into Britain in considerable numbers and proved a very popular and reliable tractor.

THE NINETEEN THIRTIES

In 1929 Fordson, which had suspended production in the USA the previous year, resumed production in Cork, Ireland, with a much improved model, the Model N or Standard Fordson. The British farmer and the public were to benefit from this, for Fordson, which moved production to Dagenham in 1933, proved to be the only substantial British manufacturer in the years up to 1945 and always produced a good tractor at an affordable price. The British-built Fordson became the mainstay of farm mechanisation; without it, farmers and the general public would have fared very badly during the Second World War.

The diesel engine started to appear on American tractors as well as in Europe; Caterpillar in 1931, Cletrac in 1933 and International in 1934 experimented with the new power unit but, apart from the superior 'slogging' characteristics of the diesel, there was little incentive in the USA, where fuel was cheap, to develop a more economical and more expensive power unit. Furthermore, with the exception of Cummins, America lacked diesel design engineers as skilled as the British and Europeans and most American diesels were based on European designs.

A most important advance in tractor design in the 1930s, which rapidly spread worldwide, was the pneumatic tyre, another American innovation. Tentative attempts at using air tyres on tractors were made in 1920, and in 1926 the French Latil four-wheel drive tractor appeared on lorry-type 'balloon' tyres, but these lacked traction on greasy soil and had to be supplemented by strakes. In the late 1920s citrus growers in Florida, concerned over the damage to tree roots caused by the steel lugs and cleats on tractor wheels, experimented with aeroplane tyres, which, not inflated, gave reasonable traction and eliminated damage. This caused a large tyre manufacturer, Firestone, to research the subject, and in 1932 they produced a very low-pressure cleated pneumatic tractor tyre, which was immediately seized on by the tractor manufacturers Allis-Chalmers of Milwaukee, Wisconsin.

Allis-Chalmers, a large conglomerate, realised that the new air tyres would boost their flagging sales in the middle of the Depression. They organised publicity stunts, such as the 'arrest' of a tractor driver for exceeding the speed limit for cars and tractor races with famous drivers, to promote the new tyre. Official tests proved that pneumatics could outperform steel wheels at virtually any job, using less fuel and causing less damage to the land. They also enabled the tractor to move easily and speedily on roads and to act as a road haulage vehicle, neither of which it could do on steel wheels; moreover tractors could return home at night to be housed under cover, instead of having to be left in the field under a sheet.

The pneumatic tyre greatly increased the scope of tractor use. By 1938 seven out of every ten new tractors in the USA had pneumatics; in Britain and Europe progress was slower, but a substantial proportion were using the new tyres by the outbreak of war in 1939. Nowadays pneumatics are universal. More than any other feature, the air tyre has made the tractor the universal tool it is today. Without it, tractors would still be lumbering about at 3 mph (5 km/h) and the huge modern high-speed and high-powered models would be impossible.

Another event of the 1930s was the introduction of hydraulic implement control on tractors. The system had been used for some years on earth-moving tractors to lift bulldozer blades and scraper buckets, but in 1934 John Deere introduced hydraulic lift for rowcrop tractors. The types of implement mounted on these machines had grown in number, size and complexity since the Farmall of 1924. These had to be lifted out of and dropped into work, and although manual lift was adequate at first, such things as mounted maize pickers and heavy multi-row seeders were becoming beyond the power of one man and a lever. 'Power lift' was the answer, mechanical in the first place, worked off the power take-off by various ingenious methods, and pioneered by John Deere on its GP model in 1928. But mechanical power was essentially inflexible and getting the power where it was needed required a complex system of wire rope, pulley and winch, which were subject to wear, rust and breakage. The new method required only a hydraulic pump, a length of hose and a ram cylinder. It was flexible, enclosed, simple and trouble-free. When John Deere introduced the system in 1934 for lifting and lowering mounted implements it was immediately widely copied, with modifications according to the whim of the designer. Some firms, like Case, used mechanical lift for many more years but eventually all conformed. Although the tricycle rowcrop tractor has never been widely used outside the USA, indirectly it had great influence on British and European design.

The best known advocate of hydraulic power control of implements was Harry Ferguson of 'Ferguson System' fame, an Ulsterman by birth and a wayward genius of many parts. Before the First World War he had worked on cars, motorcycles and aeroplanes. During the war he was an inspector of government-owned tractors under the Food Production Scheme, which operated the majority of tractors including the Fordsons. He disapproved of the conventional method of a tractor towing behind it an implement by means of a drawbar, merely acting as a replacement for the horse; he probably saw imported American Emerson-Brantingham tractors, which possessed an inbuilt mechanical lift and linkage to which implements could be attached making an integrated tractor/implement. Ferguson experimented with the idea of a tractor and implement joined as an entity, instead of separated by a drawbar. This shortened the length of the combination and made it much more manoeuvrable, enabling it to lift and reverse into corners, which was virtually impossible with drawbar implements. It also, with correctly designed geometry, added stability to the tractor and gave a measure of weight transference to it, thus improving wheel grip. His first plough on this principle appeared in 1918 and he continued to work on the design until by

ABOVE: *Munktells tractors (now BM Volvo) first appeared at the beginning of the First World War and by the early 1920s had adopted and continued to use for many years the familiar two-stroke surface ignition engine so commonly used in Scandinavian boats. Much more sophisticated and complicated than the crude Bulldog type tractors favoured by most of their continental competitors, they were nevertheless reliable and long-lived machines and could burn many types of low-grade fuel oils.*

BELOW: *The International WD40 was the first venture by any major American manufacturer into the realm of diesel-engined wheeled tractors. It used a development of the German Kamper system of starting on petrol using a normal carburettor and magneto and a sparking plug located in an extra chamber to the cylinder head proper, to which it was connected by a valve. For starting, this valve was opened, the normal inlet valve disengaged and the diesel fuel pump cut out; the engine could then be started on petrol and, when warmed up, the extra chamber and valves were cut out, the diesel pump re-engaged and the engine then worked as a normal compression ignition unit. This method gave very easy hand starting but was complex and costly and these 'split-head' engines were very liable to cylinder-head trouble, due to severe thermal stresses in the very complicated castings involved.*

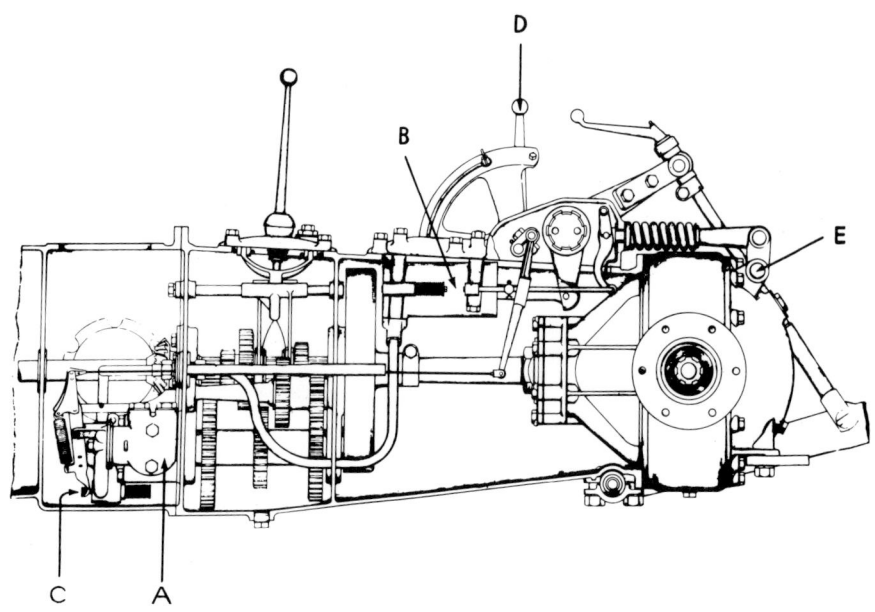

A Ferguson Model A showing the internal arrangement of the Ferguson System hydraulic lift: A, the gearbox-driven hydraulic pump; B, the pressure-release mechanism or safety device; C, the main hydraulic valve; D, the depth control and raise and lower lever; E, the pivot point for the top link of the three-point linkage, controlling the depth and the hydraulic release system through the spring and linkage.

the early 1920s he had developed a linkage-mounted hand-lift two-furrow plough specifically for the Fordson tractor. He entered into an agreement with Sherman Brothers in the USA to produce this equipment, with considerable success. Ferguson-Sherman ploughs sold in quantity into the mass market of Fordson tractors and added to their versatility, manoeuvrability and also safety, because Ferguson, noting that the early Fordson was a 'nose light' design, liable to rear up if the plough hit a solid obstruction, thereby damaging the plough or injuring the tractor driver, incorporated safety devices to prevent this. So the tractor could plough among rocks and stumps without damage to itself, the plough or the driver.

When Ford suspended production of Fordsons in 1928, to resume on a much reduced scale in Ireland the following year, Ferguson and Sherman's mass market rapidly disappeared. Ferguson determined to rethink and redesign his mounted equipment and its method of

operation. He developed a system using three flexibly jointed links, built on to the tractor and lifted and lowered by a hydraulic ram, supplied with oil under pressure by a gearbox-driven pump. He so designed the linkage that as the pull on the implement varied it automatically valved oil into and out of the ram cylinder to provide not constant depth of operation but a more or less constant draft. At the same time the reaction of the implement to the soil forces acting on it pushed forward on the third or top link to add adhesion weight to the tractor rear wheels, a force which also served to keep the nose of the tractor firmly on the ground. A safety device, also hydraulic, was incorporated to take care of the eventuality of meeting an immovable obstacle: if draft forces became excessive, for example by the implement becoming hooked on a root or rock, the top link thrust forward against its control spring and knocked the draft control valve overcentre, thus removing all hydraulic pressure from the ram cylinder and all transferred weight

The Ferguson Model A (1936-9) was the first commercially produced Ferguson System tractor and was manufactured by the David Brown Company at Huddersfield. The picture shows clearly the hydraulic three-point linkage attached to a mounted plough, the operating lever to the right of the seat and the very lightweight construction. Only about thirteen hundred of this model were built, but it served as the prototype for subsequent Ferguson System tractors.

from the tractor, which immediately just stood and spun its wheels. This prevented backwards overturning and damage to implements. These functions were controllable by a small fingertip lever working in a quadrant by the driver's right hand. The lever was pulled up the quadrant to lift the implement out of the ground and pushed down to lower it; the further it was pushed down, the deeper the implement penetrated, until a point was reached where draught reaction forces became excessive and the safety release operated, whereupon the lever had to be adjusted to give a shallower depth of operation.

In this, the simplest form of the Ferguson System, these functions only operated correctly on a lightweight tractor — one that relied on the added weight transfer provided by the linkage to be able to pull the implement at all. A heavy tractor with sufficient traction built in would ignore the signals transmitted to it and continue to heave at the implement, with possible breakage. This and the fact that the Ferguson hydraulic system was a 'work dodger', that is, it did not work at constant depth but evaded tough places in the land by easing the plough or other implement over them, militated against its universal acceptance for many years to come. Even with these shortcomings it was a revolutionary concept and Ferguson decided to build a prototype tractor to incorporate his system. This tractor appeared in 1933-4 and was called the Ferguson Black because it was painted black. Apart from the hydraulics and linkage system it showed no original features, being basically a much lighter and lower-powered version of the Fordson tractor.

Ferguson embarked on a campaign to publicise his system and to obtain financial backing to produce it but was ignored by the established manufacturers in both Britain and the USA. However, he eventually met David Brown of David

Brown Gears Ltd, who agreed to produce the tractor at Huddersfield. Production started in 1936 and about fifteen hundred were produced until 1939, when the parties separated, David Brown to produce his own tractor and Ferguson to the USA to conclude an agreement with Henry Ford, Ford to design and produce a new tractor, and Ferguson to supply his patents for the hydraulic linkage and to handle all sales in the USA. This tractor became famous as the 'Ford-Fergie', correctly the Ford Tractor with Ferguson System Model 9N. Production started in July 1939, at almost the same time as David Brown put the new David Brown Model VAK 1 on the market from his new factory at Meltham, Huddersfield, where the last few 'Fergie-Browns' (Ferguson Model A) tractors had been built.

The Ford was a vastly superior tractor to the Ferguson A. It had a good powerful engine, the same as used in the early Ford Jeeps, and became a great success. In spite of wartime restrictions nearly 250,000 were made, until Ferguson fell out with the Ford Company, which however continued to use Ferguson's hydraulic patents. Ferguson, not to be outdone, got the Standard Motor Company to make a slightly revised version of Ford's tractor design in Coventry, the famous TE20 or 'little grey Fergie'. He also took legal proceedings against Ford for infringing his patents and won. Ford revised the design to evade Ferguson and kept on making tractors in ever greater numbers as the Ford 8N.

The Coventry-built TE model sold in huge numbers all over the world, but without the Ford 9N and its virtues Ferguson could never have achieved such success, for as a *tractor* designer he was considerably less than good.

The Ford of 1939 firmly established three-point mounted and hydraulically controlled implements and before the war was over many manufacturers wanted three-point linkage and hydraulics. They could not have 'draught control' as Ferguson had watertight patents, and many modifications were used to evade them. David Brown, on producing the first David Brown tractor in 1939 after parting from Ferguson, wanted to incorporate three-point linkage and hydraulic lift, but Ferguson's linkage converged on an imaginary point and the implement, if displaced sideways, always attempted to return to its central position. This 'convergence' feature was patented and to use parallel links made the implement uncontrollable laterally. So Brown used parallel links and joined them with a diagonal bar which made it self-centring, and thus the patents were avoided.

The influence of Ferguson's designs has been vast. Virtually every tractor made since about 1950 uses Ferguson's converging linkage with hydraulic actuation, the same as that of the Fergie-Black of 1934. The safety devices of the original system have been replaced by automatic load monitoring and much more sophisticated draught regulation, and the hydraulic functions, originally confined to the linkage, now power hydraulic motors, fork-lifts, loaders and all manner of devices.

In the late 1930s tractors changed considerably in appearance owing to the popular demand for 'streamlining' and styling. John Deere, Case, International and Massey Harris, which had taken over the Wallis in 1928, all brought out 'styled' models in the immediate pre-war years. In Britain Marshall and Fordson stuck to their old designs but the new David Brown was styled and incorporated some weather protection for the driver. Continental tractors remained much as before, frequently powered by single-cylinder two and four stroke hot bulb and diesel engines, and many were at a very early stage of technical development. In addition, continental Europe lagged behind the USA in the development of pneumatic tyres, which were brought into Britain by the big tyre companies, particularly Firestone and Goodyear, whose tyres, by the outbreak of war, were little inferior to those used today, whereas European tractor tyres were of obsolete pattern.

Another American idea of the period, to increase the market for tractors, was the introduction of 'baby' tractors. These were designed as the equivalent of two horses for small farmers and, like the much bigger Farmall, to perform all farm tasks; the aim was to provide low-priced, low-powered, lightweight tractors for the peasant farmer who previously had been

The little Allis-Chalmers B, introduced in late 1937, was the first tractor in the world to be sold on pneumatic tyres without the option of steel wheels. Powered by an 18 hp four-cylinder OHV petrol paraffin engine and possessing a high clearance for rowcrop work, it was an immediate and lasting success among small farmers and had a long line of imitators and successors. Assembled and partly manufactured in England from 1947 on, it and its successors, the 270 and 272, eventually lost out to the onslaught of the Ferguson TE series in Britain.

debarred by the cost from the benefits of tractor farming. This was a major part of Ferguson's creed, but the original Ferguson failed to provide a solution because of its high price, due partly to very small production. In 1938 in Britain the Ferguson A cost £220 and also needed a new set of hydraulic lift implements, whilst the Fordson, which could use existing machines and was considerably more powerful, cost £155. The IH 10-20, superior to both, was only £220. In these days a farmworker earned £1.50 a week and corn was a few pounds a ton, and even a slightly higher cost than the Fordson price precluded widespread purchase.

Allis-Chalmers in 1937-8 introduced the famous Model B, the pioneer of these deceptively fragile-looking machines. It sold in the USA for just under the equivalent of £100 and was fitted with pneumatic tyres as standard, without the option of steel wheels, the first tractor to be so equipped. It was a notably good and willing worker and became a great and lasting success. The simultaneous introduction by Allis-Chalmers of a small cheap combine harvester which the B could handle caused the rapid spread of the combine from its previous preserve of the North American wheat belt. Other American manufacturers, including Case,

International and John Deere, copied the idea of the B and produced a satisfactory line of lightweight machines. Ford went the Ferguson way, but his version was equally good, much more sophisticated, with greater development potential.

British manufacture in this period was limited to two main companies, Fordson and Marshall, and their products were supplemented until the war by a small but steady flow of American imports, mainly bought by larger and richer farmers. The rest used Fordsons or horses. Between the wars, International, Case, Massey-Harris (formerly Wallis), Oliver (formerly Hart-Parr), John Deere and Allis-Chalmers gained a small foothold in the British market, as did Minneapolis-Moline, which in 1939 showed a tractor with a very luxurious cab, forerunner of the modern structures that at last give the driver a reasonable place to work in. European manufacturers, such as Fiat and Renault, had tried to invade the market in the early 1920s but faded away, not to reappear in Britain for thirty years. An exception was the Lanz Bulldog, which before 1939 established a small but loyal following in East Anglia. Many of these tractors worked thoughout the war and after, isolated from factory spares and service, a fine record of reliability.

This is an example, on the optional steel wheels, of the VAK 1, David Brown's first tractor made in 1939 after the split with Ferguson. Comparatively few were built, owing to Brown's commitment to war work, and it was superseded by the improved VAK 1A in April 1945.

THE SECOND WORLD WAR

On the outbreak of the Second World War in September 1939 Britain was much better prepared to increase its food production than it had been in 1914. Extensive contingency plans for British agriculture had been made, a 'bank' of Fordson tractors collected and the War Agricultural Executive Committees formed. All swung immediately into action, 'ploughing-out' campaigns were organised under government orders by the local WAECs and a contract service was created. Farmers were instructed to plough out a percentage of their grassland and sow it with cereal crops, and if they lacked the machinery to do the job they could either buy it on allocation from government reserves or the WAECs would do the work under contract. The area of arable land more than doubled during the war years: derelict land was reclaimed, drainage systems were restored, hedges cut back, downland ploughed and all manner of things done to increase home production. Farmers who did not comply with orders to farm in the new style or improve their standards were dispossessed of their land. Despite complaints about the increase in controls and paperwork, the campaign was notably effective. This would not have been possible without tractors, and the entire British tractor industry was controlled by the Ministry of Agriculture, which allocated its raw materials and other requirements and bought its products. The tractors were assigned to dealers, who could only sell to farmers possessing a ministry order to buy. Ford, the only large-scale manufacturer, rose to the occasion; in spite of bombings, blackouts and shortages of material, they kept on making more and more tractors as the war progressed.

But the Fordson, with its comparatively light weight of 1½ tons and limited power of 25 bhp (19 kW), could not tackle every job, and higher-powered and special-purpose tractors were imported from the USA in increasing numbers; and when the 'Lend Lease' legislation was passed under the influence of President Roosevelt, Britain's lack of dollars no longer prevented imports. These imported tractors were allocated and controlled in the same way as the home product.

Crawlers for agriculture and other uses came from Caterpillar, International, Allis-Chalmers and Cletrac, wheeled tractors from John Deere, Case, Oliver, Massey Harris, Minneapolis-Moline, Ford, International, Allis-Chalmers and Avery.

Few of the imports were in the Fordson class. They were mostly either higher-powered, like the Case L and LA, the J-D D, the International W-9 and the MM GTA, or of equivalent or lower power than the British-made tractors but capable of special tasks, such as rowcrop work in the sugar beet and potato areas of eastern England and Scotland, like the A-C B, the Oliver 70, the M-M RTZ, the Massey Harris 101 Jr Rowcrop and the Ford Ferguson. Fords of Dagenham had introduced a rowcrop version of the Model N in 1936, but it was never made in large numbers and, rather than have production of the invaluable Fordson agricultural and land utility models disrupted, the policy was to import rowcrop tractors from the United States.

The British-made Fordsons, performing most of the basic tasks, the high-powered American tractors, pulling and driving the much greater number of threshing machines necessitated by the expansion of the grain acreage, and the lower-powered imports, working the rowcrops and other special tasks such as heavy reclamation work for the crawlers, between them soon vastly increased the production of the depressed farmlands of Britain. No other source of power could have performed the task set by the government: steam was virtually extinct; horses did a lot of work in the war, but only because there were not enough tractors to replace them all. Once tractors were readily available again, after the war, the horses disappeared.

The tractor had achieved its all powerful place in British agriculture after a half century of effort and had, once again, helped save Britain from starvation. It was also during the Second World War that the self-propelled combine harvester first appeared in Britain, from Massey Harris of Toronto. The SP combine is, essentially, a tractor driven backwards, with a cutter bar and threshing machine built on, and it has completely ousted traditional harvesting.

Prototype Nuffield of 1946. It was scheduled for production in 1946-7 but did not appear until late 1948. It featured a five-speed forward one-speed reverse gearbox and a 36 hp (27 kW) Morris Commercial engine. This was one of very few successful post-war new makes and is now Leyland.

THE POST-WAR PERIOD

When the war ended in 1945 the number of tractors in Britain had grown enormously since 1939 and ninety per cent of them were Fordsons. In 1945, shortly before VE Day, Ford announced a new tractor, the Fordson Major, Marshall brought out its new Series 1 Field Marshall, still a single-cylinder two-stroke diesel, and David Brown introduced the Model VAK 1A, an improved version of the tractor they introduced in July 1939. David Brown had made only a few tractors during the war, but a large number of tank gearboxes. Lord Nuffield announced that Morris Motors would be producing a tractor in the near future and in 1946 Harry Ferguson's TE 20s start to roll off the lines at the Standard Banner Lane plant.

The Fordson Major had merely a different appearance, hydraulic lift facility and an improved final drive. The new Marshall was a streamlined, tidier and more powerful version of the old model M, and the Ferguson was a virtual replica of the Ford tractor of 1939. The Nuffield from Morris, which did not appear until 1948, was the only new design in Britain and it displayed little originality. So the 1940s, with two exceptions, were a sterile period for tractor design.

By contrast tractor production burgeoned everywhere, even in countries, such as Rumania and Finland, which had never made tractors before. Demand and unit production reached heights which are unlikely ever to be reached again. Many small, mostly badly run companies sprang up to cash in on the insatiable demand. By the mid 1950s they had nearly all disappeared. They were not confined to the USA, as in 1915-22, but proliferated in most western countries.

One of the technical advances of this period was the introduction by a little known Canadian tractor maker, the Cockshutt Plow Company, of the 'live' power take-off. The ordinary PTO was subject to the tractor's transmission clutch — pushing the clutch down stopped both the tractor and the implement it was driving. This was highly inconvenient, because when a driver saw a blockage, say of straw in a baler, appearing, he had to stop the tractor in an attempt to prevent it and by doing so made it a certainty. He had to decide whether the blockage would go away if he ignored it or get worse. As a result many machines could be operated only with difficulty or with much reduced efficiency when PTO driven. The solution, before the live PTO, was to build an independent engine on the machine just to drive it and let the tractor pull it along, a negation of the PTO itself and a costly and complicated remedy. Cockshutt's solution was classic in its simplicity: they merely installed two clutches, one behind the other, one to supply the power to the PTO shaft and the other to the tractor wheels; they were operated with a two-stage pedal, the first stage of which stopped the tractor and let the PTO drive continue, and the second of which stopped both. Once the system became widespread, as it did by the early 1950s in the USA and the late 1950s in Britain, the engines on the balers were no longer needed. Live PTOs, much improved, are standard fittings today.

The second technical advance was the encroachment of the diesel engine, in multi-cylindered high-speed form, into the domain of the spark ignition petrol and paraffin engines. From 1947 a number of manufacturers started seriously to consider diesel power. Oliver, in the USA, was one of the first, using its own engines, and International, which had been making limited numbers of diesel wheeled tractors and large numbers of diesel crawlers, expanded its output. John Deere, that bastion of conservative engine design, retained its horizontal two-cylinder and made a diesel, and other manufacturers followed suit. In Britain both the Fordson Major and the Massey-Harris 744 began to be fitted with the Perkins engine, and David Brown, by 1949 a power in the tractor world, was making its own engines and installing them in its Cropmaster tractor, introduced two years previously. This, apart from the special case of the Marshall single-cylinder two-stroke, was the first 'own make' diesel to be put on the market in Britain by a major manufacturer.

The diesel engine is a much more reliable and economical source of power than a spark ignition engine. It does not have troublesome electric ignition, doubly unreliable in the dirty and wet conditions tractors have to work in, and, when correctly designed and maintained, starts first time in any weather. It does not demand, like the paraffin engine, a special fuel, petrol, to start it, or an extended warm-up period. It is also a good 'puller', that is it will 'hang on' when overloaded. In addition it turns a much higher percentage of its fuel into work. Its disadvantages are that it is noisier, rougher running and more expensive than its spark ignition brother, but its virtues far outweigh its shortcomings: the proof of that is on the roads and in the fields. The diesel has swept all before it and there is as yet no threat to its supremacy as a heavy duty prime mover.

The tractor which hastened and rendered inevitable the end of the paraffin tractor in Britain was the Fordson New Major of 1952. It was offered for a time in petrol, paraffin and diesel versions, but the diesel soon completely ousted the others. It was only a little dearer, an excellent starter and very economical, and proved to be a most reliable machine. It was the start of a new era, the diesel age in farming. All manufacturers were forced to fall into line and provide diesel-engined models. Nuffield installed Perkins engines and Ferguson its own, despite opposition from Harry Ferguson, who had fought every change from straight petrol. International Harvester of Great Britain, which started manufacture of American-designed models at Doncaster in 1949, soon changed over and David Brown increased its line. Within a very few years paraffin engines were dead and diesels reigned supreme.

In the USA, however, progress was much less rapid. Cheap petrol and paraffin made the more expensive diesel unnecessary. Paraffin, known as 'distillate' in America, was the first to go, but petrol-engined tractors are, to a limited extent, still made and many are still in service. But as a result of the huge increase in tractor power during the 1960s and 1970s diesels were fitted to the majority of American tractors by the end of that period.

THE MODERN TRACTOR

The period of the vintage tractor ended in 1952 but tractor development has continued to advance since then. The most impressive thing that has happened is the massive upsurge in power. The original Fordson and other popular tractors of the period delivered around 25 bhp (19 kW), a level which altered little up to about 1950, when 35 to 40 hp (26-30 kW) tractors, like the Fordson New Major and the Nuffield, became commonplace. The ubiquitous 'Grey' Ferguson stayed at about 25 hp as did the Ford 8N in the USA. Since the early 1960s the tractors commanding the mass market have gradually increased in horsepower and the market leaders in Britain today are those of 75 to 80 hp (56-60 kW) and in the USA of 100 hp (75 kW) and above. In the USA, Canada, Australia, the USSR and other big grain farming areas tractors of 300 to 500 hp (220-370 kW) are becoming commonplace and they are gaining a foothold in Britain and western Europe. Most major tractor companies have 250-300 hp (185-220 kW) four-wheel drive tractors in their catalogues and power is likely to increase to 750 hp (560 kW) and beyond.

The modern tractor, incorporating most of the ideas of its forebears, is a highly efficient, sophisticated, high-speed machine for land working. Not so long ago 3 mph (5 km/h) ploughing was fast; now 6 mph (10 km/h) is comparatively leisurely.

In addition, the modern tractor driver can have a safety cab designed to protect him in roll-overs, soundproofing, air conditioning, luxuriously padded and sprung armchair seats, power steering and power gear shifting; radios and cassette players are commonplace and on some of the very largest American tractors closed-circuit television is fitted so that the driver can monitor his implements.

PLACES TO VISIT
The Hunday Tractor and Farm Museum, Westside, Newton, Stocksfield, near Corbridge, Northumberland. Telephone: Stocksfield (06615) 2553.
This is the most remarkable collection of farm tractors, stationary engines and agricultural equipment that is open to the public in the United Kingdom. Started in 1964 with a solitary Oliver 70 tractor by Mr John Moffitt, it is now a museum of international repute and importance.
Its primary collection of tractors is particularly strong in the very rare models of the First World War era, when tractors first became an important part of farming in Britain, and it possesses, in the famous Ivel of 1903-4, what is almost certainly the oldest tractor in running order still in existence; moreover, the Ivel is undoubtedly the prototype of the ubiquitous tractor of today.
The Hunday Museum is a fascinating collection relating to agriculture in times past and is continually growing in general interest and improving in scope.

Alscott Farm Museum, Shebbear, Devon. Telephone: Shebbear (040 928) 206.
Avoncroft Museum of Buildings, Redditch Road, Stoke Heath, Bromsgrove, Worcestershire. Telephone: Bromsgrove (0527) 31363.
Breamore Countryside Museum, Breamore House, Breamore, Hampshire. Telephone: Breamore (072 57) 468.
Doward Farm Machinery Museum, High View, Symonds Yat, Ross-on-Wye, Herefordshire. Telephone: Symonds Yat (0600) 890474.
Easton Farm Park, Easton, Woodbridge, Suffolk. Telephone: Wickham Market (0728) 746475.
James Countryside Museum, Bicton Gardens, East Budleigh, Devon. Telephone: Budleigh Salterton (039 54) 3881.
Museum of Lincolnshire Life, Burton Road, Lincoln. Telephone: Lincoln (0522) 28448 or 29864.
Naseby Battle and Farm Museum, Naseby, Northamptonshire. Telephone: Northampton (0604) 740241.
Science Museum, Exhibition Road, South Kensington, London SW7. Telephone: 01-589 6371.
Scolton Manor Museum, Spittal, near Haverfordwest, Dyfed. Telephone: Clarbeston (043 782) 328.
Steam and Countryside Museum, Sandy Bay, Exmouth, Devon.
Strumpshaw Hall Steam Museum, Strumpshaw, near Norwich. Telephone: Norwich (0603) 712339.
Yorkshire Farm Machinery Preservation Society, Burton Constable Hall, Sproatley, Humberside. Telephone enquiries: Hull (0484) 825944.